An engraving from 1745 of the battle between the English fleet and the Spanish Armada in July 1588, from a design by Hendrik Cornelisz Vroom (c. 1562–1640).

# Series 117

This is a Ladybird Expert book, one of a series of titles for an adult readership. Written by some of the leading lights and outstanding communicators in their fields and published by one of the most trusted and well-loved names in books, the Ladybird Expert series provides clear, accessible and authoritative introductions, informed by expert opinion, to key subjects drawn from science, history and culture.

*The Publisher would like to thank the following for the illustrative references for this book:*
Front endpaper © Hulton Archive/Getty Images.

Every effort has been made to ensure images are correctly attributed; however, if any omission or error has been made please notify the Publisher for correction in future editions.

MICHAEL JOSEPH

UK | USA | Canada | Ireland | Australia
India | New Zealand | South Africa

Michael Joseph is part of the Penguin Random House group of companies
whose addresses can be found at global.penguinrandomhouse.com

First published 2018
001

Printed in Italy by L.E.G.O. S.p.A.

A CIP catalogue record for this book is available from the British Library

ISBN: 978-0-718-18857-3

www.greenpenguin.co.uk

# The Spanish Armada

**Sam Willis**

with illustrations by
Paul Young

Ladybird Books Ltd, London

In the spring of 1588 England was ruled by the Tudor and Protestant Queen Elizabeth I, daughter of Henry VIII. She had been queen for twenty-nine years and was fifty-four years old, an impressive age for anyone in the sixteenth century. England had grown under her rule and was on the verge of possessing a significant international maritime empire, but was threatened by enemies from north, east and south.

Her father, once a Catholic, had split from Rome in 1533 and had made himself head of the Church in England instead of the Pope. For more than half a century tension between Catholics and Protestants had been intense, violent and sustained. Henry VIII's schism in the Church had forced a splinter into the heart of Europe which, by 1588, had become mortally infected.

During Elizabeth's reign that tension came to a head in the relationship between Protestant England and Catholic Spain, ruled by a Habsburg, King Philip II. Unlike the Tudor dynasty, which had been founded just a century before by Henry VIII's father, Henry VII, the Habsburg line was one of the most long-standing and influential of the European royal households, with roots that could be traced back half a millennium.

War between the two countries broke out in 1585 and lasted nearly thirty years, until 1604. The first crisis came in 1588 when Philip, on behalf of the Catholic Church and funded by the Pope, gathered people, ships and weapons from numerous countries all over northern Europe – including England – to create a fleet to invade England.

It became known in England as the Spanish Armada.

The origins of the Armada are many and varied but the most extraordinary of them was the repeated and direct provocation of Philip II, one of the wealthiest monarchs who ever lived, who ruled one of the largest empires ever created, by the son of a Devon farmer.

Francis Drake was born in poverty but rose in the meritocratic service of the sea, where competence was rewarded, and there have been few more competent than Drake.

In 1577–80 Drake stunned the world by sailing around it. He was only the second person to achieve this feat, and he did it in a vessel barely one hundred feet long in an age when navigation out of sight of land was mostly guesswork, when no charts existed for most of his journey, and when the world's leading navigators were Spanish and Portuguese.

In the words of the Earl of Sussex, one of Elizabeth's most important peers, Philip was 'the greatest monarch on earth, who was strong enough to wage war on all the world united', but Drake was uncowed. In the process of his circumnavigation he captured a Spanish treasure galleon, the *Nuestra Señora de la Concepción*, which made him rich beyond imagining. Six years after his return, now knighted by his Queen and sailing with her express blessing, Drake captured Santo Domingo and Cartagena, two of the most important Spanish cities in the West Indies.

The Spanish empire funded itself with silver from South America. Drake's attacks, although having a limited effect on the Spanish economy, had a profound psychological effect on Philip. He set his eyes firmly on England.

This Anglo-Spanish provocation ran both ways but where the English used men like Drake to raid Spanish territory and steal Spanish property, the Spanish used politicians and assassins to destabilize the English. Throughout the 1580s Elizabeth faced numerous plots on her life orchestrated by Catholics vying to replace her with her first cousin once removed, the Catholic Mary Stuart, Queen of Scots. Many of the plots were particularly cunning and in one, the Throckmorton Plot of 1583, the Spanish Ambassador was directly implicated.

The final straw was the Babington Plot of 1586, which was uncovered by Elizabeth's spymaster, Francis Walsingham, who intercepted and decoded a ciphered letter from Mary to Anthony Babington, the head plotter, in which Mary consented to the murder of Elizabeth.

The recurring discoveries of such conspiracies turned Elizabeth to favour the more bellicose of her courtiers. They supported war against Spain and convinced her that Mary, Queen of Scots, who many English Catholics believed to be the legitimate Catholic Queen of England, should be executed to leave no such obvious Catholic claimant to the throne.

On 8 February 1587 Mary was beheaded, the Catholic world outraged, and Philip further justified in his plans to invade England.

Philip sat at the centre of his empire, and attempted to control everything himself with a flood of paperwork. He was obsessive and intense. A deeply spiritual man, he was also austere and always wore black: he was a raven in an age of peacocks.

Philip had no specialist knowledge of naval or military affairs, though the Spanish were experienced at operating and wielding very large fleets with great success.

Seventeen years before the Armada, at the battle of Lepanto, in 1571, the Spanish had helped put a stop to Ottoman expansion in the Mediterranean. As part of a fleet of 250 ships and 80,000 sailors, they had annihilated the Ottoman fleet. Then, in 1583, when Philip fought for the Portuguese crown, the Spanish launched a successful invasion of the Azores with almost 100 ships and 11,700 men.

Both of those operations were conducted with traditional Mediterranean fleets of oared galleys. An invasion across the English Channel after a voyage through the unpredictable weather of the Bay of Biscay, fighting against English sailing warships, would require something quite different.

Philip's plan was to create a fleet of over 100 ocean-going sailing ships supported by a handful of oared craft. They would be sourced from a variety of Catholic states – Spain primarily, but also Portugal, Castile and Naples – and the sailors and soldiers from wherever they could find them. Several English Catholics signed up.

The sailing of this fleet into the English Channel formed only one part of the invasion plan.

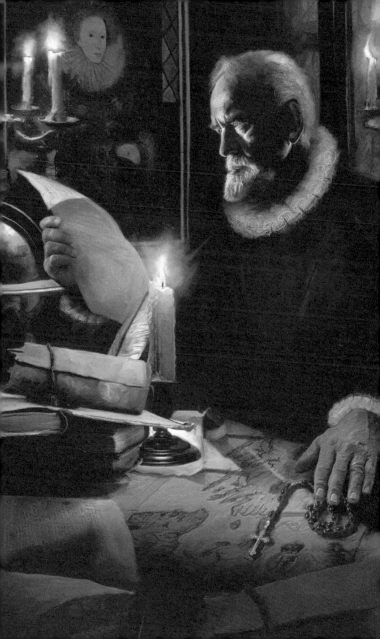

The second part involved a Spanish army under the Duke of Parma, which would wait for the fleet at Dunkirk, thirty miles from the English coast.

Parma held the key to the entire operation for political reasons. The Armada was funded by the Pope, Sixtus V. To make it clear that the campaign was not a simple exercise in Spanish aggrandizement, Philip gave Parma, a sovereign prince in his own right, command of the troops.

Parma was an outstanding soldier who had most recently made a name for himself fighting on behalf of Philip to suppress a Protestant Dutch rebellion against Habsburg rule. His troops were experienced and ruthless. In 1585 Parma and his men retook the city of Antwerp from the Dutch rebels in a relentless, ingenious and violent campaign that was followed by considered magnanimity. The English, allies of the Protestant Dutch, knew all about Parma and rightly feared him.

Philip's invasion plan was for his fleet to fight off the Royal Navy as it sailed up the Channel. It would meet Parma in Dunkirk, escort his troops across the Channel and set them on their way to London. When the Spanish landed, it was envisaged that disaffected English Catholics would rise as one to assist them.

There were, however, numerous problems with this plan.

Firstly, there was no adequate deep-water port in the Channel where the Spanish fleet could wait for Parma in safety. The Dutch, moreover, had a fleet of their own which was carefully positioned just off Dunkirk. Any attempt by Parma to move his men by sea on his own, in vulnerable inshore craft, would be suicide.

Secondly, the English fleet, which had been built up as a professional force by Henry VIII, had far more purpose-built warships than the Spanish. The English ships were fast, manoeuvrable and powerful; the Spanish fleet primarily consisted of merchantmen hired by the crown.

Thirdly, in direct contrast with the permanent and professional administration and logistical system that existed for manning, feeding and arming the Royal Navy, Philip had nothing in place to help orchestrate his plans. As a result, when the Armada finally sailed, there was an inadequate supply of *everything* in both numbers and quality. The cannon and shot were few and of different sizes; the powder was poor; there was not enough food; the food that made it on to the ships rotted; there were not enough sailors; the sailors that made it on to the ships became sick; there were not enough experienced soldiers; the ships leaked.

The Duke of Medina Sidonia, the Armada's commander, thought that Philip's plan stood little chance of success.

The English did not think like this, however. Waves of intelligence from fishermen, merchants and travellers made the threat very real.

Three times the English sailed to destroy the Armada in its Lisbon nest – on 30 May, 19 and 23 June – but on each occasion they were blown back by foul winds. Nothing could be done in England but to wait and watch the horizon. The English were terrified.

The Spanish were as frightened as the English. They knew the reality of the condition of their fleet as well as the excellent reputation of the English ships and sailors. Shortly after leaving Lisbon the Armada was forced into Corunna for more food, and a vote was taken. Nine of the ten senior officers declared the Armada too weak to continue. Philip's reply to Medina Sidonia was rather unsympathetic:

'*Pull yourself together . . . and do your part.*'

For those on board there was no doubting what situation they were in:

'*We are sailing against England in the confident hope of a miracle.*'

On 21 July they left Corunna and headed for the Channel. The voyage took ten days. Life on board was cramped, cold, austere and boring.

The Spanish soldiers and sailors slept on deck; neither they nor the English had hammocks in this period. Prayers were enforced twice daily and there were strict rules outlawing swearing, gambling and blasphemy: the holy trinity of a sailor's life thus – officially at least – denied by Philip.

A unique moment in the Spanish sailors' day happened when the ships' boys sang out the Catholic hymn 'Salve Regina' at nightfall: at this stage in the operation the soundtrack was provided by those most innocent of larks: children.

The English fleet was under the command of Lord Howard of Effingham, a statesman and courtier. He was not, however, an experienced sailor or fighter, nor were any of his senior men experienced with the particular strategic problem that now faced them. How should they meet the threat they knew was coming? Howard decided to keep a small reserve squadron at the Downs anchorage opposite Dunkirk, and sent the bulk of his fleet to Plymouth, to protect the western end of the Channel.

The first sighting of the Armada from English soil, on 20 July, was a momentous event. The dark cloud of Spanish menace that had hung over England for three years had finally manifested into a physical reality of foreign ships crewed with hostile men.

Drake, we think, was playing bowls. Did he continue to play once he received the news, claiming there was 'plenty of time' both to win the game and defeat the Spanish? Or did he rush to the harbour to force his ships to sea, to face the threat bearing down on him and to prevent his fleet from being trapped and destroyed in a lightning raid?

Logic and plenty of sensible historians suggest the latter. However, the claim that some 'Commanders and Captaines' (Drake not being named) 'were at bowles upon the hoe of Plimouth' first appeared in print as early as 1624, and the story so neatly encapsulates Drake's character that it deserves to live on, just in case it actually *is* true. Drake's proven genius – a unique mixture of fire and calm, wrath and charm, courage and patience – should remain innocent of 'doing the sensible thing' until he is actually proven guilty.

One story which certainly is a myth, however, is that beacons were lit all along the coast of Devon to warn of the arrival of the Armada, and the reason for that is important.

The long history of the British Isles is not one of strength against maritime invasion but of weakness in the face of it. In the years between the Norman Conquest and the Spanish Armada, England was invaded by sea, leading to a change in ruling power, eight times: in 1139, 1153, 1326, 1399, 1460, 1470, 1471 and 1485. The English, therefore, if nothing else, were pragmatists.

The effect of such fear was unpredictable: at worst it could cause panic and political instability. The English government therefore went to great lengths to prevent the spread of rumour. One of the ways they did this was to strictly control the warning beacons, which were only to be lit in the event of an actual landing, and with the express purpose of raising local militias to contest it.

At this stage, therefore, the beacons remained unlit and the militias remained on stand-by, but the navy certainly did not. The most striking difference between the Spanish Armada and the English navy's response to it was the time it took for each force to become effectively mobilized. The Armada took three years; the English navy, assisted by an impressive administration which included lists of all mariners in every parish in the country, just three weeks.

When the Armada finally reached the Channel and began its stately procession down that most dangerous narrow sea, the Spanish displayed quality seamanship that is instructive of the rise and subsequent strength of the Spanish Empire itself.

From the mid-sixteenth century a central tenet of English naval policy was the capture of the Spanish *flota* – the annual treasure fleet which sailed from the Caribbean to Spain. Although Drake captured that isolated treasure ship in 1579, the fleet itself was never captured. One of the reasons for this was the convoy system adopted and brilliantly executed by the Spanish.

Sailing in convoy required heavily armed manoeuvrable escorts to protect and shepherd larger, poorly armed and cumbersome merchantmen. Such station-keeping was extremely difficult with ships even of similar capability. For the Armada, a hodgepodge of small and heavy, fast and slow ships, it was near-impossible, and yet it was now executed with astonishing dexterity, the Spanish ships like so many starlings swirling from one shape to another in disdain of the wind.

They formed a crescent in which the bulk of the vulnerable transports and store ships were grouped together in the centre and protected on either 'wing' by the more manoeuvrable and heavily armed ships.

Then they waited for the English attack.

In a display of centuries-old military theatre, the first shot – a declaration of hostile intent – was fired from a small English ship named the *Disdain* before the English fell on the wings of the Armada.

They did so using a recently developed tactic in which, one by one and in line ahead, the ships bore down on their enemy, firing their bow chasers before turning away, firing one broadside and then the other, turning again to fire their stern chasers before sailing away to reload, the ships taking their turn to engage the enemy, keeping them under constant fire.

Commanders from both fleets had high expectations of this new tactic, maximizing the effect of the heavier and longer-range English guns. The effect, however, was not as expected. A mixture of English uncertainty over the strength of their foe, an unwillingness to engage as closely as possible and some fine Spanish seamanship enabled the Armada to withstand the attack and continue its journey down the Channel.

Very unusually for naval warfare, which was so often an event that occurred beyond the horizon, this play was acted out in sight of Plymouth Hoe. This battle for England, therefore, was immediate and visceral in a remarkable way, and the scars it left on the national psyche were correspondingly deep – in a similar way to those left in the Second World War by the dogfights of the Battle of Britain in the skies of southern England.

The first day of action ended with two very different events, but which were significant for the same reason.

The first was the capture of a Spanish flagship, the *Nuestra Señora del Rosario*. The *Rosario* became damaged in a collision and isolated in heavy seas. Drake saw the events unfold and, always a man to recognize and seize opportunity, broke formation from the main English fleet and took her the next morning without a fight – to the outrage and jealousy of many of his fellow captains.

The second was the partial destruction by explosion of the *San Salvador*, a heavily armed galleon. We do not know what caused the explosion – perhaps an accident, perhaps sabotage – but as many as 200 soldiers were killed or wounded when the raised deck at the ship's stern was blown off. She did not sink, however, and was also captured by the English.

These two ships provided two key things. The first was gunpowder. The English fleet had a very limited supply and by no means enough for the expected sustained and ferocious campaign. Both the *Rosario* and the *San Salvador* were stuffed with gunpowder. Between them they provided the English fleet with 229 extra barrels, perhaps a quarter of the total expended in the entire Armada campaign – at the end of which the English had completely run out. Without these twin captures, the English would have been unable to fight as they did in the coming battles.

The second was first-hand intelligence of the equipment, armament and conditions aboard two of the most important ships in the Armada, and, with Admiral Don Pedro de Valdés of the *Rosario* to interrogate, knowledge of their intentions and priorities as well.

It is certain that the English perception of the threat posed by the Spanish ships changed dramatically from this moment.

It would have been impossible not to notice that the Spanish heavy guns were mounted on huge two-wheeled carriages, which made them enormously unwieldy and very slow to reload in comparison with the short, handy, four-wheeled English gun carriages, the clear ancestors of the carriages that would be used by the Royal Navy for centuries to come.

Closer inspection would have revealed a terrible muddle concerning the guns themselves. There was no central foundry in Spain nor was there a standard system for ordnance size. This meant that the Armada guns were sourced from a variety of foundries all over Europe, each with its own distinctive type and size of ammunition.

A quick inspection of the men and the victuals would have informed the English that, with a lengthy campaign in prospect, all of the Spaniards were well on their way to starving – 'their fish [was] unsavoury and their bread full of worms', and that many of them had already fallen ill.

Much could always be learned from the cleanliness and condition of a ship. When it was boarded, the state of the *San Salvador* disgusted the English so much that they immediately abandoned it, 'finding the stink in the ship so unsavoury and the sight within board so ugly'. That smell alone told an eloquent tale of the state of the Armada: it was rotting from the inside.

After these twin disasters, Medina Sidonia decided to boost the morale and discipline of his men. He tried to achieve this by sending ships through the fleet with gallows erected on deck and hangmen standing by. His message was clear: any loss of resolve would be punishable by death.

It did little to sweep away the cobwebs of suspicion and reproach which were beginning to settle on his men. Medina Sidonia was chosen to command the Armada for his administrative experience, not for his ability to manage or lead men, and when first appointed he had written to the King begging to be bypassed, in his own words 'possessing no experience of seafaring or of war'. Nowhere is this lack of experience or understanding clearer than in his fleet's hangmen.

In contrast, Howard, the commander of the English fleet, chose to reward two key men at the next crisis point in the campaign, the battle at the Isle of Wight.

Here was Spithead, an excellent, sheltered anchorage that would allow the Spanish to land some troops. Here also was the moment when Medina Sidonia first considered abandoning his unworkable orders to make contact with Parma in Dunkirk.

The Armada headed for Spithead, still in excellent formation. Now, however, they came to be harried even more closely by the English fleet, which, also in excellent formation, forced the entire body to turn away from its landward course.

Howard was so impressed that, on the deck of his flagship the *Ark Royal*, he knighted Martin Frobisher and John Hawkins, who had taken command of two divisions of the English fleet in the day's attack. This reveals Howard for the exceptional commander that he was. Both tactful and generous, he had acute and natural insight into the minds of his men.

Medina Sidonia's plan to find some measure of respite in Spithead thus foiled, he headed out into the Channel once more, all the time moving east until he decided to anchor off Calais, only thirty miles from Parma at Dunkirk.

With the English fleet hovering on the horizon, however, those thirty miles might as well have been three thousand. The English resorted to a tried and tested tactic to root out the Armada, and one which was fully expected by the Spanish: fireships.

Eight small vessels were laden with combustibles and gunpowder, their sails hoisted, their yards made fast and their rudders lashed into position. Fuses and kindling were lit and at the last minute the crews dived overboard. The flames took hold and soon burned white-hot. With the wind behind pushing the fireships towards the Spanish fleet, impenetrable clouds of black smoke stained the sky ahead of them, an early threat of the danger they posed.

Fully prepared for the onslaught, however, a screen of small Spanish boats protecting the main fleet met the fireships and pulled them safely away. The Spanish main fleet, meanwhile, panicked by the fireships, cut and slipped their anchor cables and headed for the open sea. The formation of the Armada, the links in the chainmail that had given them their protection, was thus broken and now fell to the sea floor as so many useless rings.

The English pounced but Medina Sidonia fought a courageous rear-guard action to allow the main body of the fleet to re-form, which they executed impressively well given the panic that had taken hold the previous night.

The subsequent battle, fought in the dangerous seaway between the Goodwin Sands and the Flemish Sandbanks, was notably different from any previous action in the campaign.

The English ships fought extremely close to their enemies – some within shouting distance. At this range the gunnery was more accurate and more deadly. One ship, the *San Mateo*, received 107 direct hits. The *María Juan* sank as a result of gunfire alone, an extremely rare occurrence in the centuries of the wooden fighting ship. Shot tore men in two, taking away limbs in the blink of an eye. Shot that found their way into the ships' hulls caused foot-long jagged splinters to break off and fly indiscriminately until they found a fleshy home, opening wounds like smiles. Danger came from all directions. Falling masts and yards crushed those in their shadow, while the decks beneath the sailors' feet tilted and heaved in a hideous, lumpy swell. It was complete chaos. In the words of one Spaniard, the confusion was 'the worst there has ever been in the world'.

Two things stand out from this action. The first is that, for the first time in the campaign, the English ships successfully demonstrated their superior fighting skills, using their superior ships and their superior guns. The second is that, in spite of this and a handful of losses, the Armada retained its integrity as a fleet.

The threat to England not only remained, therefore, but this time was worse than before because, by the end of the battle, the English had fired all their ammunition.

At this stage, Howard called a council of war. This was the traditional way of making important strategic decisions at sea; it is not evidence of indecision. Indeed, the resolution produced at this meeting is resounding: if the fleet had more food and ammunition, the English commanders would pursue the Spanish 'to the furthest that they durst have gone' – the Tudor equivalent of 'to the ends of the earth'. Unfortunately, however, the ships' guns were impotent and the men starving. They would not be following the Spanish any further.

Thus, finally hobbled by the logistical challenges of naval warfare which had already been so magnificently overcome to mobilize the fleet at short notice and then fight a running battle for ten unremitting days, the English ships assumed a new passive role of simply shadowing the Armada, which was now heading north, up the east coast of England. It was nothing more than a bluff of strength – in Howard's words, 'a brag countenance'.

The Spanish, meanwhile, held their own council of war and, although the idea of returning to Calais was mooted, it was rejected in favour of 'obeying the wind'. A landing on the coast of England, although still theoretically possible, must have been far beyond their capabilities for it to have been considered at this stage. An interesting option would have been to seek shelter in Scotland – a Catholic country ruled by James VI, son of the executed Mary, Queen of Scots, with a long-established maritime industry where friendship and supplies could have been guaranteed. But it was not considered.

Instead they chose to sail directly home, around the north of Scotland and Ireland. The route is not surprising. The Spanish plotted a well-known and long-established trade route from the Baltic to Spain which ran via the north of Scotland and Ireland, and they well knew the dangers of that route, particularly the hazardous north and west coasts of Ireland. Appropriate sailing instructions were issued. Yes, they would be hungry and thirsty and tired in the four to five weeks the journey should take but, as long as the weather held, they should be safe.

The weather did not hold.

A single day after the English stopped shadowing them at the Firth of Forth a five-day-long storm struck. In such weather a sailing fleet, for its own safety, must disperse, but in cohesion lay the Armada's greatest chance of survival, as only by acting together, by exchanging crewmen, sharing supplies, repairing together and towing when necessary, could the disabled Armada make it home.

The Armada thus began to fall apart in spite of Medina Sidonia's urging, raging, encouragement and threats. And the weather never improved. The journey became, in Medina Sidonia's words, one of 'the greatest travails and miseries ever seen'.

It was only at this very late stage in the campaign that the terrible fate of so many of the Armada ships was inevitable.

It was also at this very late stage in the campaign, with the direct threat long past, that Elizabeth gave her famous speech to her troops at Tilbury, a town at a narrowing of the Thames in Essex, on the northern bank of the river, and the headquarters for Robert Dudley, the 'General of Her Majesty's forces in the South'.

The location of the speech is revealing of English vulnerability, ignorance of Spanish intentions and strategic muddle. The army was located at Tilbury to defend the Thames against an envisaged attack directly into the river. This was never the Spanish intention; rather, they planned to attack the eastern tip of Kent, somewhere around the Isle of Thanet, possibly using the anchorage of the Downs to keep the fleet riding safe while the troops were unloaded. This was where Romans, Saxons and Danes had all landed.

Elizabeth's army, therefore, was not just in the wrong location but was the wrong side of the River Thames, and there was no bridge. It was a good location for a defiant speech, therefore, on the basis that it was all she would be able to do there.

Her speech, however, was exceptional. Historians agree it was probably written by Elizabeth and that she delivered it in a carefully orchestrated display of royal theatre in which she showed herself as a leader, soldier, citizen and Queen.

She was in her mid-fifties with a wig and black teeth, but she was also dressed in white, armoured and armed and astride a horse. The effect was magical.

*'Let tyrants fear . . . I know I have the body of a weak and feeble woman, but I have the heart and stomach of a king.'*

The Armada, meanwhile, was fighting for its life. Approximately forty Spanish ships were wrecked on their voyage home and twenty-six were lost in Ireland alone. One of them, the *Girona*, was a wreck of unusual misfortune. She ran aground off Lacada Point in northern Ireland with 800 survivors on board, rescued from two other shipwrecks, in addition to her crew. Nine men survived from a total of 1,300. Aboard when she sank was the cream of Spain's young aristocratic warriors, visible now only through the remarkable treasure recovered from the wreck, which included gold chains, coins and exquisite jewel-encrusted pendants and brooches.

The archaeology of wrecks like these has utterly transformed our understanding of every aspect of the Armada, from grand strategy to life at sea, and yet only six of those twenty-six Irish wrecks have been discovered and excavated. The promise of more knowledge emerging from the depths is one of the most exciting unwritten chapters in maritime archaeology. It is certain that our understanding not only of the Armada but also of the entire period will change.

The already amazing wealth of archaeological finds, however, makes it a little too easy to focus on the disaster of the wrecked ships rather than on the exceptional feat of leadership, seamanship, courage and endurance that saw Medina Sidonia safely shepherd home sixty-seven crippled ships, crewed by starving, exhausted and injured men, in the most appalling weather conditions. Medina Sidonia may have been a disciplinarian who threatened his men with the gallows during the campaign, but that was not necessarily at odds with being an exceptional leader in these circumstances. This achievement ranks as high as any in the annals of maritime and naval endeavour.

The majority of the Spanish sailors who were lucky enough to survive the fighting in the Channel, the mortal sickness which seeped through the crews and then shipwreck in Ireland were either massacred on the Irish beaches by locals or taken into captivity before being hanged. It seems that only the wealthy stood any chance of survival as they could be ransomed.

The Armada, therefore, was a death sentence for the vast majority of those aboard. From the start to the end of the campaign perhaps 20,000 Spanish soldiers and sailors died in shivering misery, in bright flashes of violence, or in disbelief at the point of salvation.

A less well-known but equally harrowing story concerns the sailors who fought in the English fleet. They too suffered violent death, mutilation, sickness, starvation and exhaustion during the campaign, and make no mistake over its scale and impact. The *Elizabeth Jonas* began the campaign with 500 men; ten days later only 300 survived. When the ships returned to port they were, in the words of Sir John Hawkins, 'utterly unfitted and unmeet to follow any enterprise'.

To make matters worse, after the campaign, all of those owed pay or in physical or financial need because of injury or sickness were ignored by their Queen and country, which had no money set aside for such post-war care and none left to spend. Only around half of all English sailors who fought in the Armada lived to see the next New Year.

The Armada was not, therefore, a glorious event for the English, but a humanitarian disaster of unprecedented scale.

Nonetheless, the Armada *was* celebrated. We know that captured Spanish banners and streamers, so distinctive of the colourful Armada ships, were paraded around London and brought to St Paul's Cathedral, the magnificent predecessor of the current cathedral. Elizabeth also visited for a glorious thanksgiving service.

St Paul's was a significant location for such pilgrimage. The largest building in medieval England and the tallest building in the world before its spire collapsed in 1561, St Paul's was the beating heart of Protestant London. Only a generation earlier, however, before Henry VIII's split with Rome, it had been the beating heart of Catholic London. The celebrations, therefore, were the triumph of Protestant over Catholic in a monument whose history reflected the same contest and the same outcome.

The English were not the only ones to gloat. The Dutch also celebrated, and in a similar way – the battle-pennant of the *San Mateo*, which was pillaged when it ran aground off the Dutch coast, was hung in St Peter's Church in Leiden. Amazingly the banner still survives in the collections of the Museum de Lakenhal in Leiden, one of only two naval flags to exist from the sixteenth century.

These celebrations publicly papered over the cracks in England's naval defences that had been exposed by the Armada and, both rightly and wrongly, the navy found itself in a cherished position in the nation's heart. It all rather missed the point that the Armada campaign had not proved that the Royal Navy could protect England but quite the opposite: that England could be attacked and even, given a fair wind and an appropriate plan, invaded.

In Spain, Philip was enormously encouraged by the Armada campaign and wisely identified several causes of its failure, which he sought to correct. Notable amongst these was the lack of a central naval administration to oversee such a campaign. This was partially rectified in 1594 by the creation of the Junta de Armadas, an embryonic Admiralty Board which would soon be capable of launching a major naval expedition with just three months' notice. By 1592 Philip also had 40 purpose-built warships under construction and soon had a navy of 70 or 80 ships of all sizes. He also had plans to secure a deep-water harbour in Brittany from where he could launch a full-scale attack on the English coast, and he commissioned pilots to survey and explore likely landing spots in Devon and Cornwall.

This period in Spain immediately after 1588, therefore, was not one of self-blame and misery but quite the opposite – it was a golden age of Spanish naval power in which, for the first time, Philip's naval plans and resources actually began to match his ambitions.

The English, meanwhile, further antagonized Philip and undermined their own naval strength. The following spring, a flawed plan for a revenge attack, which became known as the 'Counter-Armada', was hatched. Elizabeth's strategic priority, to destroy the remains of the Armada ships lying defenceless 'all unrigged and their ordnance on the shore' in various Spanish ports, was hijacked by greed and crippled by confusion. The fleet eventually returned home with little to show for its efforts other than the fillip of making three separate landings on Spanish or Portuguese soil. During this toothless campaign, 10,000 men either died or were too incapacitated to be of any further use to the Royal Navy.

Spanish seapower, meanwhile, grew in strength. In 1595 the Spanish raided and burned Mousehole, Newlyn and Penzance from their new base in Brittany. By 1596 Philip's navy was ready for a major operation and he was now motivated by revenge. In July Lord Howard had attacked Cadiz, Spain's most prestigious and strategically significant port, and had successfully held the entire city to ransom.

Thus, eight years after the Armada of 1588, and just three months after Howard had captured Cadiz, in 1596 another Armada left Lisbon. The English fleet was in port, refitting, unable to protect the country by defending her seas. Luckily for England this Armada was blown back by terrible winds. The following year, in 1597, yet another Armada was sent out, but this also was blown back. These Armadas failed, but they were better planned, better equipped and more likely to have succeeded than that of 1588.

The real lesson of 1588 and the two subsequent failed invasion campaigns was that England, in spite of her Queen, her navy and men like Howard, Frobisher, Drake and Hawkins, was ripe for the taking.

## Further reading

Sam Willis *Fighting Ships: From the Ancient World to 1750* (Quercus, 2010)

Colin Martin and Geoffrey Parker (editors) *The Spanish Armada* (Guild, 1988)

Felipe Fernández-Armesto *The Spanish Armada: The Experience of War in 1588* (Oxford University Press, 1988)

N. A. M. Rodger *The Safeguard of the Sea: A Naval History of Britain. Vol. 1: 660–1649* (Penguin Books, 2004)